LIBER ESP III vel
DICTIONNAIRE INFERNAL

*being a grimoire of demonic incantations
as revealed in the form of poetry by*

MARIS McLAMOUREARY

to the soferim

CHRIS McCREARY & MARK LAMOUREUX

Anno Viii Sol in Scorpio – October 31, MMXVII e.n.
PHILADELPHIA

𝔑ullum 𝔖ecta 𝔈ditis

These collaborative poems
were originally published on the blog
www.marismclamoureary.blogspot.com
on a daily basis throughout National Poetry Month, April 2016.

Edited by Angelo Colavita
Cover: Martin Schongauer, *The Temptation of St. Anthony* (1470)

ISBN 978-0-9995558-0-4
Copyright © 2017 Chris McCreary
Copyright © 2017 Mark Lamoureux
First Edition 2017 Empty Set Press. Philadelphia, PA, USA
www.emptysetpress.com
Printed at Fireball Printing. Philadelphia, PA, USA
www.fireballprinting.com

TRANSPORT OF SORCERERS

Hello this one's for the cadre
of the demon-born, the überman
in the dark mirror, Pollux
to my Castor; just a kouros
on a Saturday night, no moon
in the sky but the knuckles white
& inked MOOT LIFE; this is
for Big Black playing in a dorm
room, I don't go there now
but I hear they sung
the loyal dog is dead & to sleep,
perchance to be unironically
Byronic after the appalling peal
of the blue bells & when I die
I'll go back to the attack on
the chime of the dread hour
when the dead do not rise
but prowl the long ago stage
with hip-slung basses long past
the removal of the audience.
Get them out of there
with your hydraulic lift,
this one's for the trusty steed
now just a goat with
powers of flight limited
to whims of exhausted fathers
strapped with infants in Baby
Bjorns. This is for when
there's PCP in the skunk weed &
the wallpaper starts
to shimmer. Footsteps
outside the window, a glowering
hero defined solely by the enormity
of his forehead. Inside

there are wine, women, scripts
being read on spec & to go
home, to go is to keep
nothing but his own counsel,
his keep a cold & lonely place.

GANGA-GRAMMA

Voluptuous lover or
six-limbed bongripper
lit to pop, he's drunk
on the buffalo's
blood once
again. Shiva's matted
hair hangs
like string & he dangles
from it above
the lowly women
who would cut capers
for his blessing,
simple servants of his every
whim who sing him cat's
cradles & borrowed
car keys. Play his theme song
only once before
your morning classes. Offer
him respite in the form
of a placid vase of foe's
blood, she's got four
arms to push you out
the open door
of the pagoda, into
the moist streets; the silver
bullet in the beggar's cup,
kiss it in deference
to Ganga-Gramma: dodged
second chance, one hand
to hold, three to write invoices,
one mouth to scold.

DEUMUS

Cast the first irregular stone
at the fat prince
in his high keep, keep
the huge box from whence
Deumus will arise
in the form of a great plastic
truck to trod on
your spine as any
lover would; lotus crown
redolent atop the poisoned
well, poised to snatch
the circus back from Madaama
of the blue blood; flip the bird
for a trident, your bladed
UFO, whisky in a jar, the mace-
heads of the liriope adjunct
the churchyard. Dig up the
roots & trip the cosmic flash
grenade, a blinding
white light across the
crucible before disintegration.
Hold a single
soul in a gnarled claw. Nothing
sacred, everything
severed, no stone
left unthrown.

RIBESAL

Should be a joke
but isn't: Pinocchio nose
although he might
never need to lie. Poor guy
has a dry cleaner's
hanger for a hand,
a flour barrel barely covering
his paunch, a cabbage for
his neckless head. Where his brain
should be, the business end
of a wooden spoon,
but he's still smart enough to know
all your friends are turnips
so hides in plain sight
with the kitchen appliances,
makes his home between
two hills, if you know what
I mean. A forker,
a spooner, a fooler
of militias, knights
& earnest rubes. Loves
a good opera, a giant
mug of pilsner, misdirection,
miscreancy, magic
missiles. Call for him
when the road seems
to lead back to your hovel
no matter which way
you run.

SCOX

Trade you six
settings of silver for a
healthy baby boy:
throw in dessert forks
& receive a lifetime supply of
Pampers. Trap him
in a basket, bind him in a triangle,
try to carve
him into wedges before he gets away. Never
let him near the stable or
the cats fat with infant
breath. Scox will brook
your commands so long
as your questions are phrased
in the form of an answer.
The voiceless child who wants
only to sing is given
poetry for twelve hundred
years. Not so fast, but
promises are kept
until the end of time
or such time as
the heavenly hatchet
is buried. Don't hold your breath
in your sinister hand
for eating the fruit
of the furnace. Until such time
as you will not rise,
like the flowers in the spring do,
as though they are expecting
a better world.

CERBÈRE

This dog's in the wrong
spot, draped in petticoat,
lured in cage; Pluto's booty
snatched by grey men
with whips & pocketwatches.
Cerbère hears the ticking
of their wan hearts wanting
more but paying the wrong
piper — losers, keepers,
bookmakers & moneylenders
all resplendent on tanning
benches, scorched like
chilis for the three
hungry tongues tamping
bit; horrendously & endlessly
patient & anxious to stand
before a jury of his
(or their) peers, hands
clasped behind back in seeming
penitence. Still he'll slobber
later as he laps his honey,
a lapse in judgment
hung from his neck like an engraved
Marmaduke medallion: "IF LOST,
PLEASE RETURN TO
SOLITARY CONFINEMENT." You might
drag him back, but he's never of one
mind when three heads
collide, & who's ever really
alone when they can
fight themselves for marrow
in the bone?

MOLOCH

Hide something
in each of seven drawers:
credit card, butterfly
knife, dirty magazine,
bronze flask, burner
phone, bar of soap, terrible
poem. Shake out rugs
in the kitchen, eat
the brown cloud of fine
dust like the tasty limbs
of children. A god
hungry as all the rest,
the slaughter of the innocents:
everyone is innocent
until proven worthy
of illumination. Exclaim
& exclaim again within
his hollow innards,
a strophe for every baby
he's ever churned
into butter. Tie
a bell around his neck
lest he wander too far: drum
circles to hem him in,
chicken wings &
bongos when everything's
too cheesy for his gongs
to bang.

9

XAPHAN

Can't blame a guy for trying
to blowtorch the pearly gates,
melt down St. Peter's
fillings & sell them on the
deep web. If you're
going to douse yourself
in gasoline, might as well
bring the bellows so the whole
world burns with you. His
Zippo's engraved with his
bellows & hell was just
a great heap of sticks before
Xaphan arrived. Cooks your
cocktail, fries your soul
like a druggie egg. Pulls
the alarm at vespers.
Long live the pan
that hovers above
his smoldering pate, poached
& plated, your very world,
on flames, a freight train
running through the middle
of the reeking pit.

FURFUR

Fillet four frogs
for Furur; find fresh
freesia fronds for
fermenting. Flatten
fraternities, feign flatulence.
Forsake frumpery; freeze
fruit, feeling fairly free
for fisticuffs. Fly fast,
first fasting for four
fortnights. Fucking
Furfur forfeits foolishness
for frottage, frank
fellow, frisky fiend, forget
forsaken family, find
feminine forks for feasting,
famished foreman. Finally,
forbidden festivities find
form. Focus, Furfur. Ferret
for foxfire, fulsome
feuds forborne for foreseen
futures. Foyers frame
forays forth from fools
for fortune, forbiddance,
forgetting. Foreskin's
furnace fungal from
fapping's furor fatal for
fourteen favored furcifers'
flesh for fantasy's
final farcical fossils.

ABRAXAS

Late in the game, an inscribed stone unearthed, its hymn
written of the basilisk born outside the skin
of time. The cock crows & so we steal
toward the figure kneeling in baptism or benediction, crown
askew, robe open,
runes carved into chest as a ward or charm.

Second time is the charm,
his crocodile tears a sort of hymn
to Abraxas who knows of lack & yet shall open
the heavens as easily as peeling skin
from a grape. As the crow's
flown round, reeling in place when steel

meets steel,
so shall even the archons come to harm.
Scepter or sword absolve no one, only the crown
pushed forth shrieking on the battlefield: caul washed from him
leaving a trove of emeralds once we skin
his feathered little torso, flay & open

the still-beating heart. Scrawl the covenant, O pen
of the capillary; render nerves to steel,
stone my heart & sting my skin
with thine goggling eyes. Charm
the snake of the spine, tap him,
her, him, her, duck, duck, crown

of thorns; a stack of black crayons
on the table papered for grim repast. Open
the bloodwine casks, let him
begin the dread toast. Still
& cold sit the many guests, charmed
by the glamor of Abraxas' kin.

Fill the skins
of sable angel leather; wear their crowns
of gold for bangles, their charms
& portents; open
the steel
gates to their croaking hymns

& Fibonacci-frenzied skin, open
fire O horn-crowned steel-footed
Abraxas: hymn-harmed & many-eyed.

AZAZEL

Mark the heretic,
marry the women but
don't abandon the escape
goat. Let's get one thing
straight, it says here
he's an angel of complete
removal. Does not bear
but rather eats your sin
like venison left out
on the counter
overnight: a clean
slate, yet mouth's
dry as a desert. He'll
gift you ranseurs,
spears, cherry-flavored
lip gloss. Listen
when he says it's time
to strike, to parlay,
to run or pucker up.

BARBATOS

Follow the lowing of the cattle,
the tweets & re-
tweets of red-breasted robins
to find him. His dominion

diminished & old
enough he must employ his sturdy
longbow as his walking stick,
his hounds still

sniff out treasure
buried by wizard & pirate
alike. Follow him
across the glen & he will

show you wonders tucked within
the gnarling of his grey-
white beard: glass beads,
bright marsh lights

aglint with cold fire;
his flicker will tell you
the way through
the mazy wood to

the fair ring where
fireflies alight sans
merci, mercurial,
for the poor & you are

the poor; lantern of
no warmth, Barbatos'
baubles useless but
stultifying. Lose

your self & dance
forever. Heaven
for the better sorts – this
is your place, this is the place for you.

STOLAS

& Stolas partook of his
medicinal herbs, & he consulted the stars,
feet became claws &

wide his eyes opened in awe: chakras
blossomed & a marsh
he saw,

a Coleman stove & a cabin
built from logs & its doorway adorned
in precious stones. & Stolas

felt himself scroll sideways, flightless &
unfeathered from ruining bridges
in West Virginia – he knows no stars

are evil, no omens ill but rather
the manchildren are ill. Run
away from home,

spend a few nights in the museum
of the bog – thundering & slurping,
the peat will hold you safe

as houses, for a thousand years
until astronauts cut open your stomach
to dissect the rat you had for lunch.

PICOLLUS

By the great men & women
& the many others
whose effusions may placate
colleagues squatting
in the next cubicle. No gods,
no masters, but sincere
belief in mercury retrograde
& wager a hanged
man's hand: tallow for a candle,
a gambit to seal the contract,
dread business letter format,
attachments: a photo
of a drowned bird, a dead man's
W-4 soaked in WD40 to balm
the valve of heaven & this
hell of gruesome boilerplate
& endless self-assessment, that burble
is Picollus chortling in his temple
for he has a temple & you
have to find a way out
of this: third time's a harm;
quit meeting like this, someone
is out for blood & the king
is dead & the queen is dead
& the angel who guards the door
is dead.

AMON

To reconcile friends
who have fallen out
of the suicide doors
of the lowriding rig,
play *Viva Hate*
forwards & fill a bottle
of blue soda with Black
Velvet; suspend
the wriggling effigy
of the punk rock high
school love triangle
above the gaping
beak of Amon, you
did the right thing
back then now
let go & let the needle
plough the groove, *icebreaker*
shall sail right through
cold mirror slicked
with spit — take an origami
dove & shove it
in the flame: a goof,
a gaffe lacking
logic as fishhook caught
between canine teeth.
Demon most solid,
give me serpentine
persistence, let me wriggle
or writhe while my
memory's still a parking lot
peopled with enemies & long
forgotten friends whose
exits left impressions,
tires put to
pavement put to my
backside & my denim
jacket clove & smoking.

FORCAS

Cut not your hair
& grab your spear,
get out of the wagon &
onto your pony
& ride; Forcas knows
the virtues of herbs
& precious stones, the names
of the cyclopean builders
who plopped the fulsome hills
down on your sleeping
burg; he teaches logic, esthetics,
chiromancy, pyromancy
& rhetoric. He can make a man
invisible, ingenious & well
-spoken in cabal or committee,
drag the minutes with incendiary
rude wit, the real
deal, stopper of bucks,
starter of riots. Just ask him
& he'll tell of rebellions
unquelled even as his stallion
bucked & whinnied. One hoof
in front of the other & his
legions at his heels: listen,
learn, his lessons
tarnished as a stranger's plate
gauntlet found by the
fork in the road.

BAËL

Triskaidekaphilia adds an umlaut
to your Yahweh, got to kiss
an army of spiders until
you get a toad, a cat & man-
splainy old elf; eat the cookies
of the underworld & stay
for a time. Baël makes a bed
for you to lie in. Prince of lays
just could not conjugate correctly
to save not his but the lives
of a whole ark of kittens. Next time
take a plane, old man with a fear
of the sky; the heretic flies
the unassuming skies, a whole
swarm of same blots out
fertile crops curated for next year's
food blogs. Sixty-six train
stations & for each a conductor
who believes he's invisible. Watch
him cower behind the counter
crying himself hoarse. The abyss
has no bottom, but he's got numerous
pamphlets charting alternate routes.

ASTAROTH

Wednesday's child is no fun
at parties, handles snakes
as though they were a knapsack
of fetid anthologies. Get
on your rat & find your way
to the cabal, ugly angel,
Astaroth, seller of books,
maker of deals. Just a sheep
in bat wings; was born that way.
Oh Hell, you're nothing
like an antihero when you
claim that the Fall just happened
to you while you were busy
playing Parcheesi, minding
your own with three
of your beasties. When
you meet him, bring
a clothespin for your nose
to block his fetid odors.
Compliment his superpowers,
ask after his sister, clutch
the silver ring hidden
in your waistcoat
until you're free to leave.

CAYM

Of shrill birdspeak
make a lecture
on despair, despair,
despair.

Black wings,
black eyes,
red beak & wicked
blade. Baked

in a pie like
desiccated grapes
on the breast
of Pallas. Knows
what you did,
evermore learned

than the dove,
dullard, drops
pebbles in the mouth
of willing
delegates & wills them

to break with convention,
woos them with
promise of spiced
wine & loose women,

wind in immigrants'
faces, a million whining
planchettes scraping their names
across the ledger
of eternity's corporate boardroom
& casino
penthouse suite.

BELZEBUTH

Hits heavy, sells out
coliseums; just a guy
on a wall alive
with black pixels,
aloft on Jolly
Rogers. In the neighborhood,
under the bridge,
in the basement
with vaseline & the cloak
of a lamb. In the compound
of eyes, doors never closed.
There never was a lock
that could hold Belzebuth
at the wrong end
of a one-way street. Hold
counsel with the bag
of bones, larva in the flames
of blood red
candle. Older than men,
repulsed by them, fed by their
left hands under blacklight in his
big corner office, each
buffalo wing another offering,
another stain on his zebra-
skin rug. Lately he's
doodling during staff meetings,
zoned out & scrolling his Instafeed
for health goths & hot young
witches with low self esteem. The astral
made material, he'll project
next quarter's earnings,
liquidate his Swiss savings accounts,
delegate the melting down of this
shitpile's keys on his way
out of town.

RAHOVART

Hand on your
shoulder & abundant oil
for his lantern, climb in that basket
& leave your treasures
behind. His boots
are made for plodding, stomping,
finding fault lines
in the face of the Father,
the Son & the poltergeist
who showed up one day
asking for plates to break.
Rahovart plays with dolls
& you are the doll,
curmudgeon bludgeoned
by his stick, off his fiery
lawn, his dread record
collection, his foul commemorative
manikins, his tour posters, his home
office full of flayed
souls.

ANDRAS

Say an owl with the body
of a man; angels' wings
stolen from the doves.
Who giveth the foot-
soldiers wings? Why fly
when you can ride the black
-hearted wolf. Sœur
of this cord,
discarded servants rife
for the reaping of the great
scimitar of the crescent
moon. Death to you
ends in spring, anxious
buds tight little
fists. Say no more, walk
away in silence
& don't come back
until you've got five sticks
of dynamite, a cudgel
fashioned from an ex-
lover's brand-new bedpost,
a shotgun sawed off
& filled with birdshot.
Await the signal then
gouge the eye, sweep
the leg: Andras
isn't the man to fight
for your honor
but he'll survive to flay
another knight &
fight another
day.

MYCALE

Caller of the jade
rabbit, blood
queen, O Luna winking
for Lumiere rockets.
Crepe dangles an ectoplasmic
wattle from your
maiden's cone — Mycale
cast your spell on the
rustic moor, rod in hand.
Night majorette, moonlight
on the pert folds of
your witch's shift. My lady
of etched stars, nothing
but a singer of songs.
Just a girl
in a swamp. Just
a mage maging
for her magic moon,
not a man but a big
bauble, a porthole
to the mother & then the crone,
pomegranate seeds dropped
from their aprons as the tides
tug her in for a kiss.

YAN-GANT-Y-TAN

I.

Light the first candle
for the road-killed, red
eyes of taillights; swimming
fins of Yan-gant-y-tan
all in chrome at the back.
Black road like a garrotte,
the silk cravat on the cadaver.
Tie one on; he's got plenty
light for those with none.

II.

Light another for the wronged;
just could not see a way
through to the other
side of the bad bog. Sat
down in the dark water.
Brought you along, to have
& to hold out for dawn
who never came.

III.

Three's a charm, a token,
an Italian horn for hirsute
torso of suitor done gone
in the inky night of abandon.
Cut the rug until tendons
ruptured: farmer's daughters
his Achilles heel, feet of dead
bunnies under his thumb.

IV.

Four is for sorrow & no tomorrow
for any young buck
dumb enough to walk these paths
at dusk. Find a hollow,
climb a tree or tallest peak;
steal the stash of pyrite, feed your tongue
to house cats, beg one last favor
of another dead god.

V.

Place the butcher knife in the turf,
blade facing up. Burn
the fifth votive, then pass the last
roach to our lonesome traveler:
he'll pry open a box
of shotgun shells, fling pellets
at the campfire. When the sun
rises, piss on the embers.
Scatter the ashes. Begin to dig.

www.ingramcontent.com/pod-product-compliance
Lightning Source LLC
Chambersburg PA
CBHW072057040426
42447CB00012BB/3161